CW00740212

ON THE
·S·P·O·T·
GUIDES

AIRBRUSH

MAINTENANCE

PETER OWEN & JOHN SUTCLIFFE

·OUTLINE PRESS·

AN OUTLINE PRESS BOOK

© OUTLINE PRESS (BOOK PUBLISHERS) LIMITED 1989
First published in Great Britain in 1989 by
Outline Press Limited, 115J Cleveland Street
London W1P 5PN

ISBN 1.871547.00.8

This book was designed and produced by
THE OUTLINE PRESS LIMITED.

Typesetting by Midford Typesetting Ltd.

Printed and bound by Grafoimpex, Zagreb, Yugoslavia.

·C·O·N·T·E·N·T·S·

INTRODUCTION

Treat your airbrush right, and you'll find it one of the most well-behaved of instruments.

In the main, things only start going wrong when you stop looking after your airbrush. If you fail to clean it after every use or forget the simple routine maintenance procedures, your airbrush will let you know in no uncertain terms - and you can't blame the tool.

This 'On-the-Spot Guide' explains all you need to know about airbrush maintenance and repair, to help you get years of trouble-free use out of your instrument. You'll learn how your airbrush works, which is essential if you are to maintain it in tip-top condition: how to go about regular and routine preventive measures: and how to recognize and remedy the most common faults.

Why do you need this 'bible' in the first place, when your airbrush more than likely came with a manufacturer's instruction sheet? Well, in our experience, most of these bits of paper only give you the most basic information. They're often badly translated from another language with vague and confusing instructions, and they miss out more than they include. Besides that, if you're like most airbrush owners, you'll either drop paint on them in the first week or lose them down the back of a drawer.

With this guide to hand, you have a permanent, comprehensive source of reference that clearly and simply shows you what - and what not - to do.

FIRST THINGS FIRST

The first thing you should do upon picking up this guide is to use it to identify exactly what type of airbrush you own.

We're not talking about the brand name or particular model, but the essential type - single-action, double-action, fixed double-action, turbo or whatever. Every kind of airbrush used worldwide is to be found in these pages, so yours should be readily recognizable. (Different makes of the same type may vary slightly, but each type group works on the same principle).

Even if you already know which type you own, there are other things you should find out now. It may sound silly, but if you don't know what you've got down to the last part, you're not in a position to look after your airbrush properly.

For example: nozzle identification

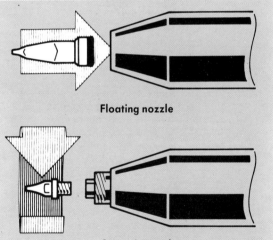

Floating nozzle

Screw-in nozzle

Take nozzles, for instance - that's the bit at the front of your airbrush. Can you say now whether your airbrush is fitted with a floating nozzle, or a screw-in nozzle?

If you can't, you need to find out because different nozzles require different maintenance.

So identify your type, know your parts, and you won't go wrong.

chapter one

KNOW YOUR AIRBRUSH

The airbrush is an
air-powered paintbrush.
To make it work its
magic, you need two further
elements: paint to put in it,
and compressed air to blow
through it. Then it's
up to you.

HOW YOUR·AIRBRUSH WORKS

All airbrushes, however simple or sophisticated,
work on the same basic principle.

There are two channels, one for air, one for paint.
When compressed air is forced through the narrow
air channel, it speeds up and its pressure drops. The
air is travelling at its fastest as it passes through the
airbrush nozzle, and the drop in pressure at that point
draws liquid (held at atmospheric pressure) up the
paint channel. As the paint is drawn into the air
stream, it atomizes and becomes an even spray.

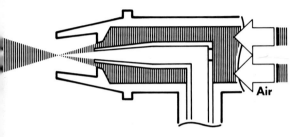

Compressed air forced through air channel

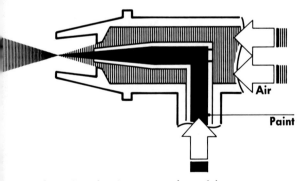

Paint drawn into the air stream and atomizing

This spray would not be controllable if the airbrush
didn't have a needle in the paint channel. The needle
can be moved backwards or forwards by the
operator: when it is fully forward it blocks the supply
of paint altogether. As it is pulled back, it allows an
increasing amount of paint to flow through, creating
a wider spray.

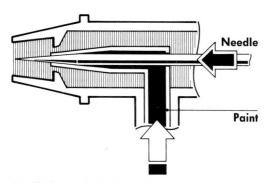

Needle

Paint

Needle forward blocking paint supply

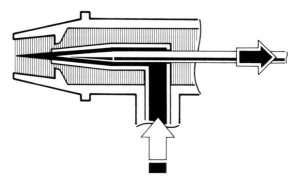

Needle pulled back allowing paint to flow through

THE TWO TYPES OF FEED

With all airbrushes, paint is fed into the body by either suction or gravity. Either way produces an equally successful result in terms of spray quality, so the only considerations that need to be taken into account are practical ones.

In suction feed models, the paint is stored in a cup or jar below or to the side of the airbrush body. When the air rushes through, the paint is sucked into the body by the force. The advantages of suction feed are that generally the jars have a large capacity, and can be easily swopped over when you want to change colours. The disadvantage is that the bulky jars can get in the way, especially when you're attempting some close detail work.

In gravity-feed models, paint is stored either in a cup

above or to the side of the body, or in a recess contained within the actual body itself. Like Newton's apple, paint drops into the airbrush through gravitational force. The advantages are that gravity-fed airbrushes are usually better-balanced and more manoeuvrable, being lighter and more compact. The only disadvantage is that cup capacity is a bit limited, although refilling doesn't present a problem.
In the following pages, we shall take each of the five airbrush types, and examine them in detail.

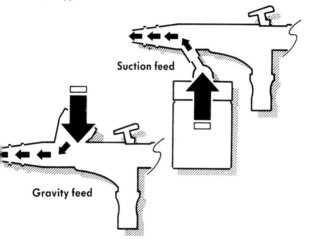

Suction feed

Gravity feed

WHO DOES WHAT WITH AN AIRBRUSH

Airbrushes are used by all sorts of people, all over the world.
At one end of the scale, airbrushing is the means by which often highly-paid commercial illustrators earn their living. At the other it's the way in which enthusiastic model-makers choose to put the finishing touches to the plastic kits they've assembled. Fine artists use them to create works of art, ceramicists to paint pottery, set designers to embellish stage backdrops, fabric painters to spray T-shirts, photo-retouchers to restore photographs, spray-painters to customize vehicles.
Amateur or professional, beginner or seasoned veteran, they all have one thing in common: the need to treat the airbrush with all due care and consideration.

THE FIVE TYPES OF AIRBRUSH

Essentially, there are five different types of airbrush. We have excluded air markers, simple modellers' spray guns, and the large capacity spray guns used in vehicle workshops. Not because they don't serve a useful purpose - which they do - but because they cannot be categorized as airbrushes in the true sense of the word.

The type you choose can be governed by two simple factors: what you intend to use your airbrush for, and how much you can afford to pay for it. To a certain extent, skill doesn't enter into the equation: to be honest, you're just as well off starting to learn with a double-action airbrush, as with a single-action. Odds are, if you buy a single-action you'll be hankering after a double-action within a couple of months anyway. Having said this, absolute beginners should avoid the Turbo: it's a magnificent beast, but uncontrollable in all but the most expert hands.

1. Single-action, external mix   pg. 12

With single-action airbrushes, when you depress the lever, a pre-set amount of paint is released. You can vary this amount on certain models by mechanically adjusting the nozzle/needle assemblies, but this means you have to stop spraying. External mix means exactly what it says: air and paint meet at the very tip of the airbrush and only have time to atomize into a large dot pattern before they hit the surface you're spraying.

2. Single-action, internal mix   pg. 14

Again, only a pre-set amount of paint is expelled when you press the lever. The difference here, though, stems from the internal mix factor. Paint and air are introduced to each other within the airbrush body, and this gives them the time and space to blend together well into a fine, consistent spray.

3. Fixed double-action   pg. 16

With double-action airbrushes you have greater
control over both the air flow and paint supply. In
'fixed' models - of which there are very few available
- the ratio of air and paint is pre-set. The lever only
goes in one direction, first activating the air and then
the paint. Although you cannot play around with the
two while actually spraying (switching from a lot of
air and a little paint to vice versa), you can on most
models pre-set the instrument to give different ratios.

4. Independent double-action   pg. 18

These most popular of models are fitted with a genuine
two-way lever: press it down for air, pull it back for
paint. This facility allows you to control air and paint
supplies totally independently, so you can achieve a
vast range of different effects and finishes. It gives
you the versatility and flexibility to vary everything
from the width of lines to the opacity of paint.
All you have to do is synchronize your pressing and
pulling to arrive at the exact effect you're looking for!

5. Double-action Turbo   pg. 20

This highly sophisticated, temperamental airbrush is
an independent double-action model, with one extra
feature that gives it it's prowess - a turbine that
rotates at up to 20,000 rpm. How it works will be
explained later, but the advantage to users is that the
actual speed of the spray can be controlled. In the
right hands, this unique facility enables the artist to
produce the very finest of work.

SINGLE-ACTION, EXTERNAL MIX

This type of cheap and cheerful airbrush is particularly popular among hobbyists - people who don't see airbrushing as an end in itself, but as a good way of decorating the objects they make. For instance, it's more than adequate for putting the finishing touches to models, ceramics or fabrics. It can be used for graphics, especially if you're spraying flat colours and are not looking for a slick finish or fine detail. However, close inspection of your

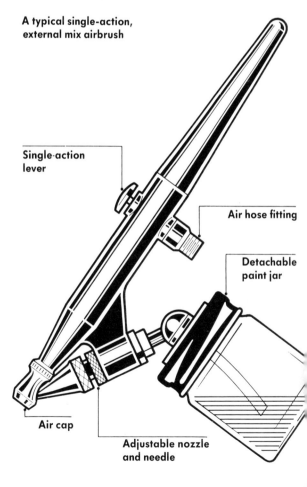

A typical single-action, external mix airbrush

Single-action lever

Air hose fitting

Detachable paint jar

Air cap

Adjustable nozzle and needle

work would betray the fact that single-action external mix models produce a coarse, stipply spray, and are prone to spattering.

Basic Operation

You simply depress the lever to control the air flow - the paint is then drawn from the paint reservoir by suction. The air flow is directed onto the needle, which is carrying the paint supply. The two only meet at the head of the airbrush, so they do not intermingle very well, which accounts for the coarse nature of the spray. With some models, interchangeable air caps and nozzle/needle assemblies are offered, which enable you to spray varying amounts of paint - and therefore various spray widths. It's useful to have this flexibility, but the problem remains that you obviously can't switch while you're spraying. If you're attempting something a little ambitious with graded tones, you'll find it's a stop-start process.

These limitations are perfectly acceptable to model-makers and the like, who also appreciate how easy these airbrushes are to use and maintain.

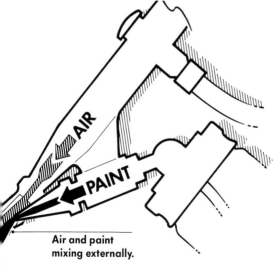

Air and paint mixing externally.

The external mixing of air and paint

SINGLE-ACTION, INTERNAL MIX

Again, this type of airbrush is mainly used by enthusiastic hobbyists looking for a polished finish. It's not too difficult to use, so there's little risk of ruining a model, ceramic vase or whatever at the last hurdle. It's also good for lettering if you're after a professional finish for posters or signs.

It scores over external mix models on spray quality. Paint and air meet in the body of the airbrush and mix together thoroughly before exiting at the tip. The

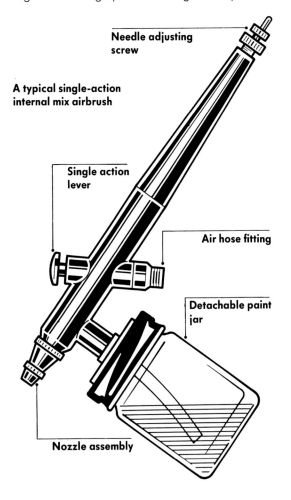

Needle adjusting screw

A typical single-action internal mix airbrush

Single action lever

Air hose fitting

Detachable paint jar

Nozzle assembly

result is a much smoother, more consistent finish on the sprayed surface.

A word of advice: if you're thinking of buying a single-action internal mix airbrush, check out some of the lower-cost double-action models at the same time. You'll find that there really isn't too much difference in price, which would tip the balance in favour of the more flexible and versatile double-action style.

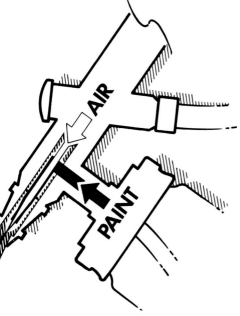

The internal mixing of air and paint

Basic Operation

Press the lever down, and you'll activate the air source and at the same time release a pre-set amount of paint. The needle setting regulates the paint supply, and on many models this can be altered by means of a needle adjusting screw located on the rear of the airbrush handle. This allows you to vary your spray width, though you're inviting trouble if you attempt to continue spraying while you adjust the needle position.

DOUBLE-ACTION, FIXED

There's only a handful of these, probably because they fall into a sort of airbrush no-man's-land between single-action types and the more popular, more versatile independent double-action models (see over).

They are used by some illustrators, mainly for accurate, technical renderings which don't call for the kind of effects found in more graphic, creative work. The actual spray quality is excellent, and given patience, you can achieve very fine, precise results.

A typical fixed double-action airbrush

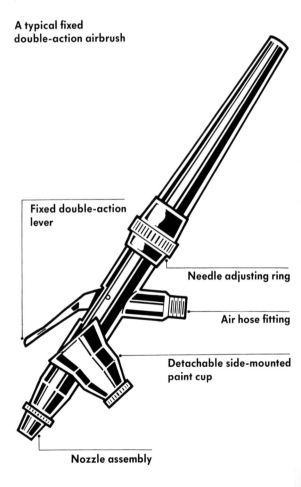

Fixed double-action lever

Needle adjusting ring

Air hose fitting

Detachable side-mounted paint cup

Nozzle assembly

Basic Operation

In double-action fixed models, the lever goes either up and down only or backwards and forwards only, depending on the make. Let's assume we're talking about an up-and-down lever.

Press it down until at halfway it releases air only. Keep pressing, and the paint supply comes in (that happens when the lever has been depressed enough to push the needle backwards). While you do have control over both paint and air, the ratio

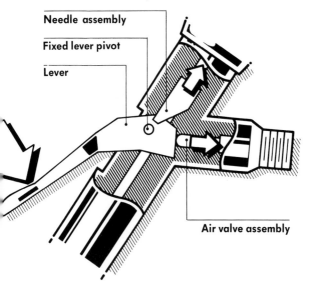

Needle assembly

Fixed lever pivot

Lever

Air valve assembly

When the lever is pressed air and paint are released in a fixed ratio, the further down the lever is pressed the more air and paint are released and dispensed.

between them is fixed. You can't, for instance, combine a lot of paint with a little air: the lever only goes in one direction, controlling two elements, so your power of control is limited. You can keep changing the ratio by pre-setting the instrument, and some models feature a needle adjusting ring for variable spray width.

Relatively easy to master, fixed double-action types are suitable for those who don't aspire to total control over an airbrush.

DOUBLE-ACTION, INDEPENDENT

This type of airbrush is the one most favoured by professional illustrators and retouchers. Many different models are available, some with varying features or accessories, but they all give the artist complete control over both air and paint volumes. This control makes independent models extremely versatile: given the manual skill and dexterity of an experienced user, they can be tamed to produce the intricate, accurate detail needed for technical or medical illustration, or imaginative, innovative graphic treatments for advertising and design work.

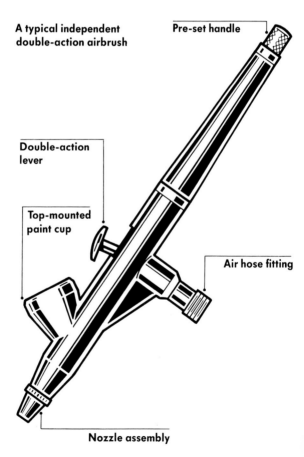

A typical independent double-action airbrush

Pre-set handle

Double-action lever

Top-mounted paint cup

Air hose fitting

Nozzle assembly

Obviously, they're not just for professionals. If you're serious about airbrushing and prepared to take the time and trouble to master the instrument, an independent double-action model is your wisest choice.

Basic Operation

It sounds simple: press the lever down for air, pull it back for paint. The further it goes down, the stronger the air force, the further it goes back, the greater the amount of paint. You can juggle with the two, mixing the proportions at will.

In practice, it isn't so simple. The lever is touch-sensitive, so obtaining the right blend of air and paint is a delicate balancing act. You'll find it comes with experience.

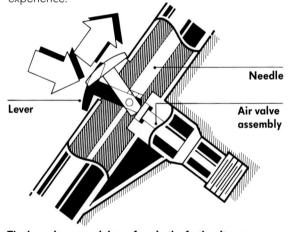

Needle

Lever

Air valve assembly

The lever is pressed down for air, the further it goes down, the stronger the air's force. Then by pulling the lever back paint is introduced, the further it goes back, the greater the amount of paint.

Different models have various different devices that can be used to fix or limit how far back the lever can travel. Some have what's known as a pre-set handle, others feature a cam ring or adjustable locking screw. These devices which lock the needle in a retracted position are particularly useful if you need a uniform supply of paint and set spray width - when you're stencilling letters for instance.

DOUBLE-ACTION TURBO

This weird and wonderful tool is in a category all by itself, and is used by commercial illustrators of the highest calibre and also by some fine artists.

It is essentially an independent double-action model, but it incorporates one major feature that sets it apart from all other airbrushes - a turbine that rotates at speeds of up to 20,000 rpm. The artist can control the speed of this turbine, and thus the speed of the spray.

In expert hands, this facility can be exploited to produce the extremely fine lines necessary for detailed, delicate work. Subtle tones and tints can also be achieved, which explains why the Turbo is favoured by artists with a more 'painterly' style.

No way is it a beginner's tool. Sensitive and sophisticated, it demands the very highest level of skill. Aim for it, but above all don't take on the Turbo until you're ready for it: it might put you off airbrushing forever.

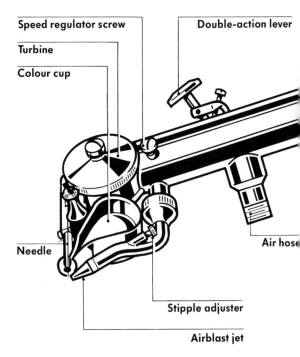

Speed regulator screw

Double-action lever

Turbine

Colour cup

Needle

Air hose

Stipple adjuster

Airblast jet

Basic operation

Hardly 'basic' but here goes.

First of all, before you pick up the Turbo, it's interesting to know what goes on inside it. The turbine is linked to an arm which moves the needle backwards and forwards at high speed. As it does so, paint is drawn onto the needle via a tiny corridor along which the needle oscillates. The paint is then driven into the path of the air jet, and the clean needle returns, at very high speed, to collect more paint.

That's the principle: the operating technique is, in part, similar to that needed for conventional double-action airbrushes. You pull the lever back for paint, press it down for air. In addition, you have to master two further controls: the turbine speed control, and a stipple adjuster within the air nozzle, which determines the volume of air passing through. If all this sounds complicated, it's because it is.

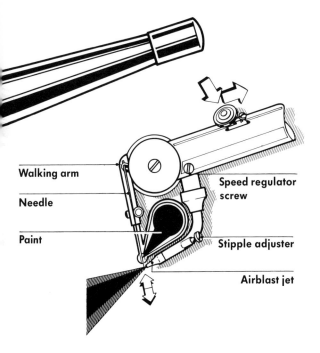

Walking arm

Needle

Paint

Speed regulator screw

Stipple adjuster

Airblast jet

chapter two

KNOW YOUR AIR SOURCE

Compressed air doesn't emerge out of thin air. It has to be generated by an air source, then fed into your airbrush. Sources can be as simple or sophisticated as you choose.

ALL YOU NEED TO KNOW ABOUT AIR

When your airbrush doesn't work properly, it isn't necessarily the instrument itself that's at fault. It could well be your air source. Just as we human beings depend on a regular supply of good air to function properly, so does your airbrush.

The ideal air source should supply a constant, regulated flow of air that is free of both moisture and oil. Like it or not, you're going to have to pay to get an air source that does just that. There are some cheap alternatives, but they perform like cheap alternatives. You'll get by with them, but if you're a good artist with a good airbrush, they'll let the side down.

Having said that, if you don't use your airbrush often, and only then for undemanding applications, there's little point in shelling out more than you need on an over-specified air source. It's a case of horses for courses.

THE SIX TYPES OF AIR SOURCE

Don't rush headlong into buying an air source. In particular, beware of false economy: for about the price of 30 propellant cans you can get a diaphragm compressor, which will last you longer and serve you better. Ultimately, though, you can only buy what you can afford and the following six sources embrace all budgets, albeit offering varying qualities of air.

The spare tyre

Certainly cheap, if not free, but you won't get an even supply of air. Make sure the tyre is still on the wheel, and inflate it by foot pump. You'll need a thread adaptor, a control valve and an air hose to go with it.

Plus points
☐ Low cost
☐ No mains power supply required

Minuses
☐ Inconsistent air supply
☐ Heavy and cumbersome
☐ Dirty and damp

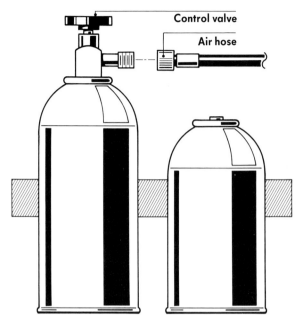

Control valve

Air hose

Propellant cans

Often used by beginners, propellant cans generally
deliver a reasonable supply of air. One obvious
drawback is that once half-empty, the pressure
begins to drop and you don't get a constant flow.
You'll need a control valve (either a straightforward
on/off type or a more sophisticated adjustable valve
allowing you to vary the pressure) and an air hose,
and there's one optional extra which you may find
useful - a metred valve that tells you how much air is
left in the can. This will prevent the maddening
situation of the can running dry when you're in full
flow, which can spoil your artwork.

Plus points
☐ Low cost option for occasional users
☐ Convenient and portable
☐ No mains power supply required

Minuses
☐ Not economical for the regular airbrush user
☐ Air pressure deteriorates as can empties

The CO2 cylinder

These large air cylinders - like those that are used to pump beer - provide a consistent stream of air. It's important that you obtain a tank from a specialist supplier who can advise you how to set it up correctly. Normally, you have to pay for the tank in the first place, but thereafter only for the air. Required accessories are a pressure regulator, control valve, measuring gauge, an air hose, and a trolley or stand for moving your cylinder around.

Plus points
☐ A long-lasting source of steady air
☐ No mains power supply required
☐ Maintenance free

Minuses
☐ Initial expense of cylinder
☐ Awkward to move around
☐ Requires a lot of space

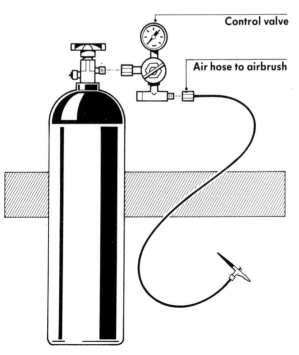

Control valve

Air hose to airbrush

Diaphragm compressor

There are several different makes of diaphragm compressor, all relatively inexpensive and perfectly adequate for the enthusiast who is not looking to produce detailed or highly-polished work.

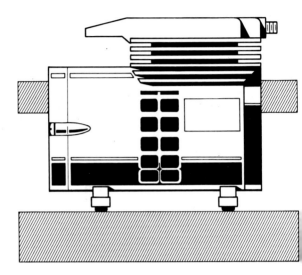

When you switch on one of these compressors, a fan sucks air in, the diaphragm compresses it and then syphons it into the air hose. This is not a smooth action, so you don't get a smooth air flow: it's prone to 'pulsing'. Your spray will be uneven, most noticeably if you're filling in a large background. There is a way round this problem, but it involves using a battery of accessories. By the time you've paid for them all, you probably could have bought a small storage compressor, so observe the golden rule and think carefully before putting your hand in your pocket. These accessories are:

Footswitch A very useful accessory because to prolong the life of your machine you should switch it off whenever you are not spraying and a footswitch located on the mains lead within easy reach will mean you are not constantly getting up and down to switch the compressor on and off.

Pulse eliminator This serves the purpose of a holding station for air between the compressor and air hose. It goes some way towards solving the pulsing problem, and incorporates an integral pressure regulator and gauge.

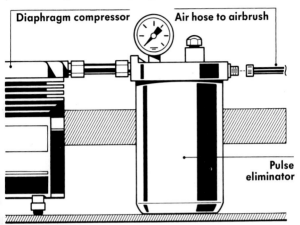

Diaphragm compressor   Air hose to airbrush

Pulse eliminator

Moisture trap (see Air Accessories) This comes complete with a pressure regulator and gauge. If you're going to use your compressor for long periods, it's a good idea to mount this away from the main body of the compressor - moisture traps don't work at full capacity when hot. A cooling hose and bracket are required in this case.

One further thing: it's essential when using this type of compressor that the airhose adaptor used with it incorporates an air bleed-off valve or has a small hole drilled in it to prevent a build up of air in the airhose when the airbrush is not being used.

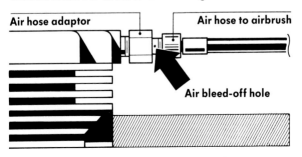

Air hose adaptor   Air hose to airbrush

Air bleed-off hole

Plus points
☐ Relatively inexpensive
☐ Maintenance free, no oiling required
☐ Durable and lightweight

Minuses
☐ Needs a power supply
☐ Tendency to overheat in lengthy use
☐ Pulsing, unless accessories are used
☐ Noisy

The small storage compressor

In this type of compressor air is stored in a tank and then by various methods fed through to the air hose, at a constant pressure - eliminating the problem of pulsing. Consequently, the quality of air supply is excellent. These are piston machines, relying on a motor to pump air into the tank, and there is a choice of manual or automatic versions. Manual models can be irritating, because you have to switch the

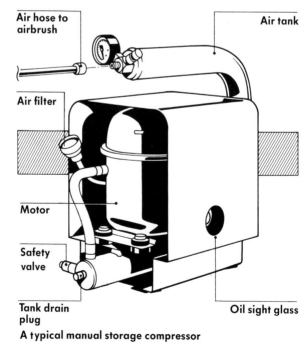

Air hose to airbrush

Air tank

Air filter

Motor

Safety valve

Tank drain plug

Oil sight glass

A typical manual storage compressor

motor on and off constantly, although this can be eased by the fitting of a footswitch. With automatic models, the motor cuts in and out by itself so you can carry on spraying without interruption. The automatic models are well-specified, with a pressure regulator, moisture trap and gauge as standard equipment. The only optional extra you might like to consider is an oil mist filter (see Air Accessories).

Plus points
☐ Excellent air quality
☐ Compact and silent
☐ Reliable and durable

Minuses
☐ Comparatively expensive - but you get what you pay for
☐ Inconvenience of manual versions

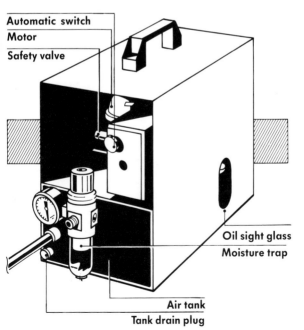

A typical automatic storage compressor

The large storage compressor

Fully-automatic and with a high capacity tank, this type of compressor is the professionals' favourite. In many ways it's no different from automatic small storage compressors, only it can service up to four airbrushes at the same time. It's built for heavy-duty use and incorporates all the features you'd expect. Again, the only optional extra you should think about if it is an oil-filled compressor is an oil mist filter.

Plus points
☐ Excellent air quality
☐ Fully automatic, with high capacity tank
☐ Services up to four airbrushes simultaneously
☐ Reliable and durable
☐ Silent and surprisingly compact

Minuses
☐ It is the best, so it costs the most
☐ Repairs, if necessary, should only be undertaken by qualified service engineers

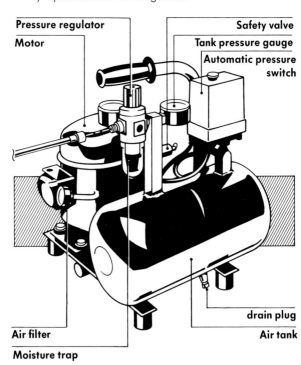

Pressure regulator

Motor

Safety valve

Tank pressure gauge

Automatic pressure switch

Air filter

Moisture trap

drain plug

Air tank

AIR ACCESSORIES
Air hoses

Not so much an accessory, as an essential. It's the
vital link between the air source and the airbrush.
Hoses are available in various lengths and there's no
point in buying one that's any longer than you need
as it will only get in the way. If the connectors at the
end of the hose aren't the same size thread as those
on your airbrush and air source (the two will
probably have different size threads anyway), you
should have no difficulty in obtaining a suitable
adaptor. You've a choice of three types of hose.

Air hoses

Clear plastic hose Lightweight, cheap and
transparent, so you can spot moisture forming in it.
Also, however, the most easily damaged.

Braided rubber hose Strong and long-lasting,
the traditional choice.

Curly coil A relative newcomer, but fast gaining
popularity because it's light, compact, tough and
modern.

Adaptors, connectors and manifolds

Almost any airbrush can be linked to any air source thanks to the wide range of threaded adaptors available. An alternative that's growing in popularity is the quick-release connector. Instead of having to fiddle around with spanners every time you want to make a connection, you simply push and twist these couplings for an airtight seal.

If you plan to operate more than one airbrush off your compressor you'll need a multi-outlet manifold. These are available to accommodate up to five airbrushes.

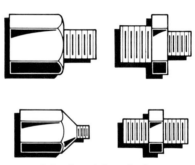

Selection of thread adaptors

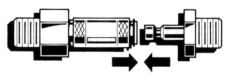

Quick-release connector

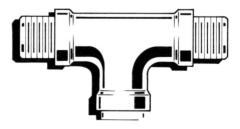

Two-way outlet manifold

Moisture traps and air regulators

Most compressors feature built-in moisture traps, but not all. If you don't have one, you need to get one, because there's no other way of preventing moisture creeping up the air hose, into your airbrush and ultimately onto your artwork. You must drain off the moisture from the trap regularly, and change the filter inside it annually.

Similarly, you can't sensibly get by without an air regulator for adjusting the air pressure. If your compressor doesn't have one fitted as standard, you can buy them individually or as a combined unit with a moisture trap.

Moisture trap

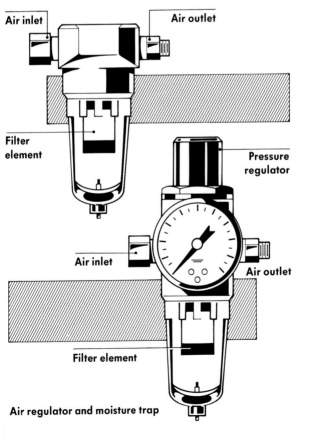

Air inlet

Air outlet

Filter element

Pressure regulator

Air inlet

Air outlet

Filter element

Air regulator and moisture trap

Oil mist filters

When small or large oil-filled compressors reach a high temperature, they can give off an oil mist. Like moisture, this mist can travel up into the airbrush and out onto the artwork. As a preventive measure, it's advisable to fit an oil mist filter.

AIR SOURCE MAINTENANCE

The only air sources that require maintenance are compressors, and even they demand relatively little attention.

To start off on the right foot, if you're buying a new storage compressor make sure it comes with a test certificate. This ensures that the manufacturer has put it through a proper pre-delivery inspection. Once you get it home always keep it in an upright, level position and allow air to circulate around it when in use.

If your compressor ever develops a fault, stop using it immediately. As with any machine, you'll grow accustomed to its general behaviour, so at the first sign of abnormal overheating or any unusual noise, switch off. Unless you're qualified to tackle repairs yourself, return it to an authorized dealer who can diagnose and cure the problem.

DIAPHRAGM COMPRESSOR MAINTENANCE

There are just a couple of things you need to check, and a couple of 'warning' signs.
1. Always check that the bleed hole is completely clear. Unblock if necessary.
2. Visually check the electrics every now and again.
3. If your compressor overheats, you're probably using it for too long a period. Rest it more frequently, but if it continues to overheat, get it checked out.
4. Towards the end of its life, your compressor may start to emit a high-pitched whine. Take it in to a service agent for assessment.

STORAGE COMPRESSOR MAINTENANCE

The procedures are simple and should be followed to the letter. Don't take any short-cuts, because you'll only saddle yourself with more work or more expense later.

Routine procedures - weekly or after use

1. Drain off any moisture from the outlet filter - push up spring-loaded plunger or screw plunger at the bottom of the bowl.
2. Inspect air intake filter and clean or replace if necessary.
3. Drain moisture from reservoir tank by opening the drain off screw at the base of the tank - after unit is switched off and air removed from tank.
4. If an oil-filled compressor, check oil level and top up if necessary, using only the type of oil specified in the manufacturer's instructions.

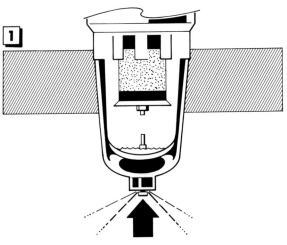

Weekly maintenance

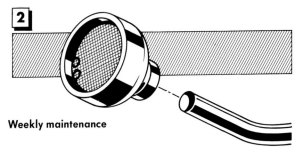

Weekly maintenance

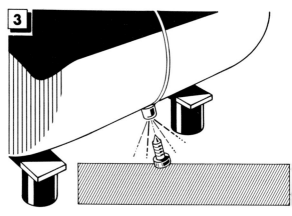

Weekly maintenance

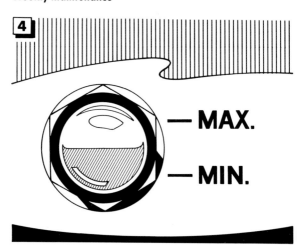

Weekly maintenance

Routine procedures - annually

1. Check the entire system for any sign of air leaks -
look and listen along the pipes and hoses, and at the
connections. Air leaks can be fixed by simply
tightening the joint, checking or replacing the seal, or
using a plumbers'sealing tape.
2. Visually check the electrics - if there is a problem
get an electrician to look at it.

3. If an oil-filled compressor - change the oil. To do this remove the sight glass carefully and tilt the compressor draining the oil into an old tin or jar, replace sight glass and refill with recommended oil.
4. Replace any outlet filter elements and clean bowls with warm soapy water.

Annual maintenance

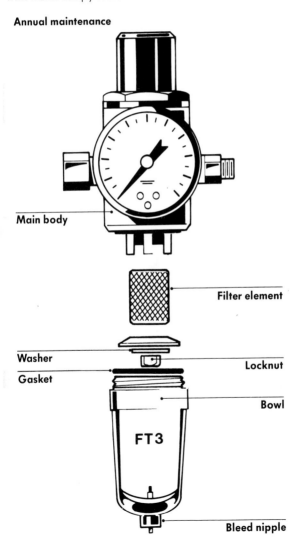

Main body

Filter element

Washer

Locknut

Gasket

Bowl

FT3

Bleed nipple

Small diaphragm compressor and *single-action external mix airbrush.*

Small diaphragm compressor *with a pressure regulator and a basic double-action airbrush.*

Small storage compressor *with moisture trap, pressure adjuster, and footswitch, and a double-action airbrush.*

Small automatic, silent compressor *with air storage tank, regulator gauge, moisture trap and two-way outlet manifold, and two professional, double-action airbrushes.*

Large silent compressor *with four-way manifold and quick-release fittings, supplying four professional double action airbrushes.*

EQUIPMENT COMPATIBILITY:
Six suggested combinations

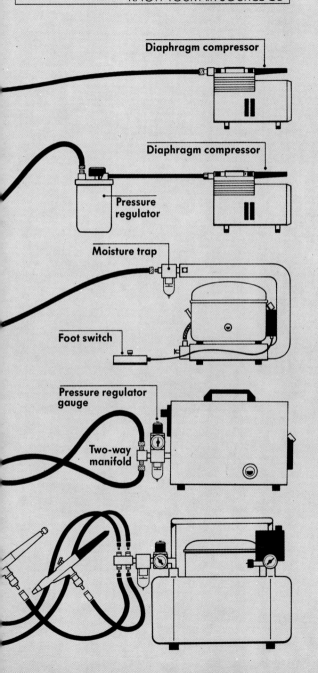

Diaphragm compressor

Diaphragm compressor

Pressure regulator

Moisture trap

Foot switch

Pressure regulator gauge

Two-way manifold

chapter three

HOW TO OPERATE AN AIRBRUSH

Operating an airbrush is like driving a car. After a while it becomes second nature, but first you must learn to co-ordinate your movements. This chapter will get you on the road.

MACHINE FAULT, OR OPERATOR ERROR?

Everyone knows the old proverb that a bad workman blames his tools. With the airbrush, all too often the tool takes the blame when the real problem is poor airbrush control by the operator.

This chapter sets out to teach you the basic handling rules. Follow them, and you'll avoid the simple errors that can plague the beginner's progress. If you do stick to the rules but still seem to be having difficulty obtaining a good clean result, then perhaps you ought to have your airbrush checked out.

PREPARING TO SPRAY

The first thing to do is to organize your system. Attach your airbrush to your air source using the hose, and switch on the source at the mains if necessary (we're stating the obvious here perhaps, but there are people who seem to think that an airbrush is somehow self-propelled). If you're using a compressor with a pressure regulator set it to the normal operating pressure of 30 psi (2 bar).

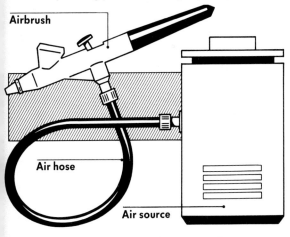

Airbrush

Air hose

Air source

Next, try holding your airbrush in two or three different ways, to find out which suits you best. There is no one correct way, although many users are most comfortable holding an airbrush like a pen - held between thumb and second finger with the forefinger on top controlling the lever. Once you've found your

Loading paint with a brush

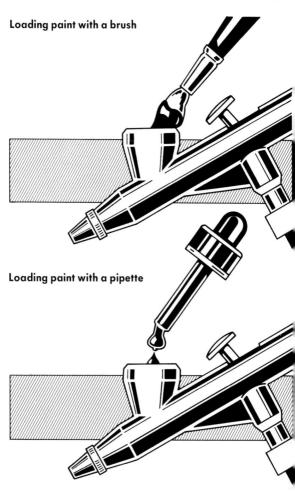

Loading paint with a pipette

preferred position try a few dry runs without paint just to get a feeling of the lever and how the air force responds to it. When you're confident that you're ready to go, load the paint. Whatever kind of paint you use - we recommend inks or watercolours which can be used straight from the bottle - make sure that it's a milky consistency. It should flow through a close-mesh tea strainer, rather than drip. You may have to mix some paints with water to achieve this consistency.

OBTAINING A SPRAY
SINGLE-ACTION

As discussed in Chapter One your control over single-action models is limited. Press the lever down, and you'll obtain a pre-set ratio of paint and air.

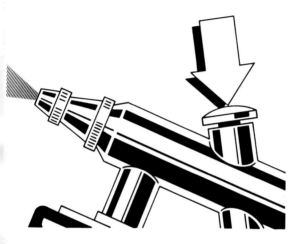

DOUBLE-ACTION, FIXED

Remember, the lever controls both paint and air, but only to a fixed ratio. With some models you have to pull the lever back, with others you have to press it down - you can't do both. You can actually vary the amount of paint expelled on certain types, by pre-setting a needle adjusting ring.

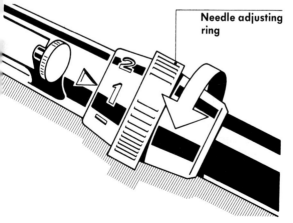

Needle adjusting ring

DOUBLE-ACTION, INDEPENDENT

You'll remember that the lever controls air and paint separately. Press down for air, pull back for paint. The further back you pull the lever, the more paint you're calling up from the reservoir - and the wider the spray.

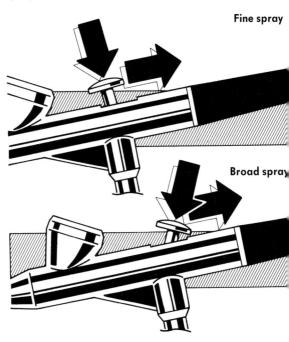

Fine spray

Broad spray

DOUBLE-ACTION, INDEPENDENT
THE GOLDEN RULE
Air on first, air off last.

With double-action models, the key is to start off with air only.

The situation you must avoid at all costs is 'paint on, air off' - that is, the lever pulled back but not depressed. In this case, paint accumulates on the needle and sits there waiting for the air to arrive. When it does, the paint simply splats onto your artwork in a big splodgy mess.

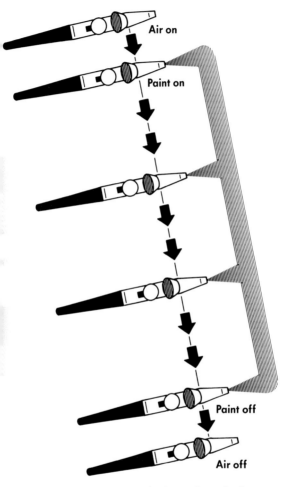

Always, but always, press the lever down before you
pull it back, and when you stop spraying make sure
it's fully forward before you lift your finger off.
Here's a good tip: if you're spraying a line, don't start
by pointing the airbrush at the exact spot where you
want the line to begin. Start earlier, moving smoothly
towards the target point with air on only. When you're
in line with the point, pull back for paint. Similarly, at
the end of the line, switch off the paint but carry on
for a second or two with air on only.

VARYING THE SPRAY

Initially, while you're coming to grips with your airbrush and trying to master its touch-sensitive control, you should practice freehand spraying. Hold your airbrush about 3in/7.5cm from the surface and just spray away - you'll soon pick up the behavioural patterns of your instrument.

After a while, try varying the spray by moving your airbrush closer to the surface, and then further away from it. The closer to the surface, the finer and stronger the line: the further away, the broader and weaker.

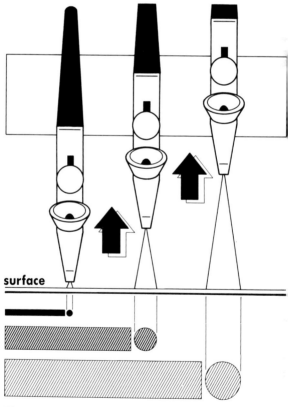

surface

This exercise is pretty elementary of course, but it's all part of the vital 'getting to know you process' between you and your airbrush.

BEGINNERS BEWARE!

There are four classic handling faults that generally afflict beginners, and if you only encounter three you're doing well. Remember, these problems are caused by operator error, not mechanical faults.

FAULT	POSSIBLE CAUSES
Spidering	Working too close to the surface Too much paint, too little air Paint on, air off.

Flooding	Paint too thin Too much paint, too little air

Spitting at start of stroke	Paint before air

Spitting at end of stroke	Lever released suddenly instead of being closed off gradually

FOUR SIMPLE EXERCISES

Never rush anything with the airbrush. Tackle things patiently and build up your confidence gradually. Don't expect to 'get the knack' overnight. It could be a while coming, and it's best you know that and settle for it at the outset. Besides, we believe in the philosophy that says the hardest skills to acquire in life are also ultimately the most rewarding. Now that's quite enough of that.

The following four exercises will teach you the basic strokes that are used in all airbrush art.

Exercise one: Flat tone

We're aiming here for a solid block of colour. You'll need to build it up gradually, because as you'll see, one pass doesn't get you very far. The end result should be flat, even and uniform in every way. No furry edges, no mottled areas, no marbling.

1. Draw up a 2in/5cm square on a sheet of thin card, using pencil and ruler. Cut the square out with a scalpel.
2. Lay the sheet on top of a piece of art board, and tape it down.

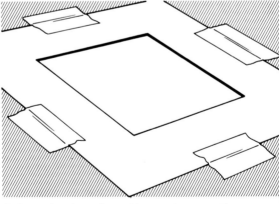

3. Spray backwards and forwards across the square, onto the art board below. Hold the airbrush 3in/7.5cm from the board, and remember to start your strokes before the edges of the square. It doesn't matter in the slightest if you spray over the top 'masking' card. You should overlap each stroke,

and leave the paint to dry after each complete layering of the square. Remove the mask temporarily if you want to inspect your square in its stark reality, as you're building it up.
4. This is what you're aiming for - a flawless solid square. It looks easier than it is.

Exercise two: Graduated tone

Here we're going to start with solid colour and then simply fade it away to nothing. The smoothness of the fade is all-important.
1. and 2. As Exercise One
3. In your head, divide the square horizontally into thirds. Holding your airbrush about 4in/10cm from the board, spray backwards and forwards across the bottom third of the square. Towards the end of this third, start lifting your airbrush away from the surface in an arc. Continue to lift and arc through the middle third, while also releasing the paint and air flows. Get this right, and you won't even have to touch the final third: the overspray will have completed the job for you.

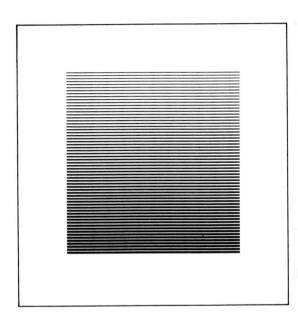

Exercise three: Freehand dots and lines
Dots
Just have a go at spraying a small, clean dot.
A splat? Well, that's too much paint and too little air
and you'll just have to keep on trying until you've got
the balance right.

Lines
The trick here is to avoid blobs at the start and finish
of your line. The best tip is to start moving into the line
without either air or paint, and to continue moving
out of your line again with air and paint off. The
smoothness of your movement is critical, and rigid
stop-start action should be avoided.

Joining the dots

If you can do dots and lines, what can be the problem with joining the dots? Just you try it and see! Pencil in a grid of 1/2in/1.5cm squares on your paper, and airbrush your dots at the intersections. Then try connecting the dots diagonally.

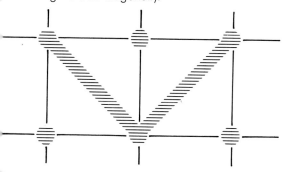

Exercise four: Spraying a circle

First mask off a square as in Exercise One. Now your objective is to spray a circle within that square, without filling in either the middle of your circle or the corners of the square. Those are the areas that attract overspray like a magnet.

You should hold your airbrush about 2in/5cm from the surface, and begin a circular movement with air on only before introducing the paint. You'll have to go over the circle three or four times to achieve strength of colour - try to follow the same line each time.

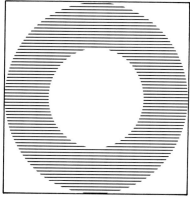

Once you've mastered these exercises, you can consider yourself in command of your airbrush. There's still a lot to learn, but this basic grounding in the essential techniques of airbrushing is a sound platform on which to build.

How to spatter and stipple

This isn't an exercise as such, but the spatter effect is one of the mainstays of airbrushing and a good spatter should be part of your repertoire.

There are three ways you can spatter and stipple.

1. You can use a purpose-designed spatter cap, if there's one available for your particular model - ask your dealer. To fit a spatter cap, first retract the needle then remove the air and needle caps and carefully screw in the spatter cap, reset the needle and now your airbrush will spatter automatically. To vary the size and effect, you can either adjust the air pressure or alter the consistency of your paint without thickening it excessively.

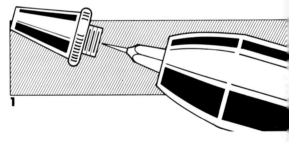

2. If there isn't a spatter cap for your model, and your model is fitted with a screw-in nozzle simply remove the needle cap and nozzle cap. This should give you the right result, and again you can experiment by varying the air pressure and paint consistency. Be very careful, however, as your needle is totally unprotected with the caps removed.

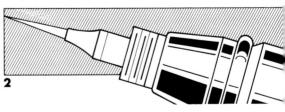

3. This method breaks all the rules, but it works! Leave your airbrush exactly as it is, but lower the air pressure: now pull the lever right the way back for maximum paint flow, then very slightly press it down for a minimum of air. Not textbook stuff, but if you like the effect - which is quite light - then there can be no arguments.

chapter four

TOOLS, MAINTENANCE & CLEANING EQUIPMENT

A simple motto: be prepared. Acquire all of the equipment listed in our inventory — it shouldn't be expensive — and have it to hand at all times. The worst time to discover you need something is when you haven't got it.

THREE KITS AT LOW COST

You don't need a huge amount of equipment to maintain your airbrush properly, you just need the right things. We've broken down the inventory into three parts - the Tool Kit, the Cleaning Kit, and the Lubricating and Sealing Kit - and while you may feel you can survive without every single item listed, it shouldn't break the bank to assemble them all. It's a good idea to keep each of the three kits in a separate box, because you won't always need them at the same time.

THE TOOL KIT

Firstly, you may or may not be aware that some airbrush manufacturers can supply special tool kits for servicing and repairing specific airbrushes. These consist of purpose-designed tools for negotiating delicate parts like diaphragm assemblies and valves. Unless you plan to service your own airbrush - which is a complex task in itself - you don't need a special kit. They can be expensive, and our advice would be to direct your funds towards buying, say, a good compressor rather than special tools. Servicing is best left to qualified agents, but if you are determined to have a go yourself, check out firstly whether your airbrush does actually need special tools for servicing (some don't) and secondly, how much the kit costs. The following Tool Kit is ideal for routine maintenance, and apart from the nozzle spanner and reamer it consists of items that should be readily available from any good hardware store.

Nozzle spanner

Some airbrushes are supplied with a small nozzle spanner and where tt is is the case, no other spanner should be used for unscrewing the nozzle.

Reamer

Again a reamer is supplied with some makes of airbrush. These sharp, thin tools - similar to needles - are used for cleaning airbrush nozzles. If your particular airbrush came with one, use it carefully. If it didn't, don't worry - other, simpler ways of cleaning your nozzle will be explained later.

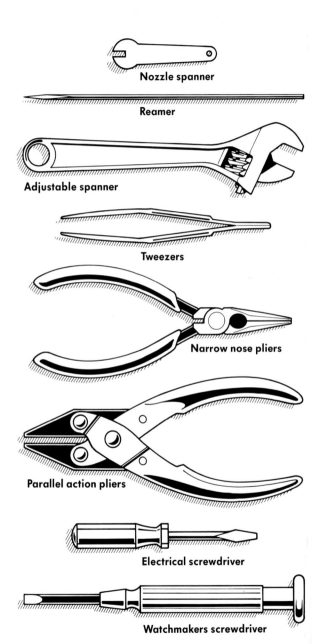

Nozzle spanner

Reamer

Adjustable spanner

Tweezers

Narrow nose pliers

Parallel action pliers

Electrical screwdriver

Watchmakers screwdriver

Adjustable spanner
Get a decent quality spanner that doesn't have an annoying 'give', needing constant adjustment.

Tweezers
A pair of tweezers is useful for extracting parts like air valves and washers from inside the airbrush.

Pliers
Two pairs: parallel-action for stripping-down and assembly jobs, and narrow-nosed for gripping small, hard-to-get-at components. Be careful, because too firm a grip with pliers can damage the soft metals in airbrushes. Consider wrapping the jaws with tape, thin aluminium sheet or plastic hose.

Screwdrivers
The screws found in airbrushes are small, so you'll need corresponding screwdrivers. Small electrical or watchmakers' types are ideal.

THE CLEANING KIT

Bowls and jars etc.
A selection, from small, individual portion jam-jars to squeezable washing-up liquid bottles filled with water.

Cotton buds, tissues etc.
You probably can't imagine what you need cotton buds, pipe cleaners and kitchen paper for, but rest assured you need them.

Brushes

Small, stiff paint brushes are useful for cleaning airbrushes, as are angled toothbrushes.

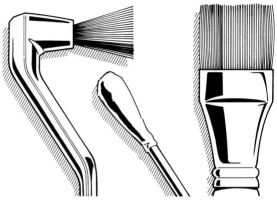

Solvents

You need a solvent to flush out your airbrush, and your choice will be dictated by what kind of paint you spray. You'll make life easy for yourself if you use water-based paints like watercolours or inks, because they can be cleaned by water. More stubborn paints like acrylics or oils require special solvents, some of these contain ammonia. You have to be careful here, because if you leave airbrush parts to soak in strong solvents to shift reluctant paint residue, you may irreparably damage those parts. If you're not happy using watercolours or inks, always check with your supplier as to the solvent required for the paint you are using.

A light abrasive polish

This will serve two purposes. It can remove corrosion build-up on metal components, and cosmetically clean the metal body of your airbrush.

Finally, there's one more item that very much falls into the 'optional extra' category. It's an ultrasonic cleaner for use on stripped down airbrushes. If you spray a volatile paint that necessitates comprehensive, frequent cleaning of internal parts, these cleaners are both convenient and effective. Most specialist airbrush suppliers should be able to supply ultrasonic cleaners and solvents.

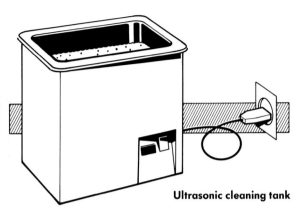

Ultrasonic cleaning tank

THE LUBRICATING AND SEALING KIT
Petroleum jelly
The best lubricant for moving parts in an airbrush is petroleum jelly, available from any supermarket or drugstore.

Jointing compound
If you seem to be having difficulty achieving airtight seals anywhere in your set-up, try solving the problem with a standard jointing compound.
Failing that, drip melted pure beeswax onto the joint.

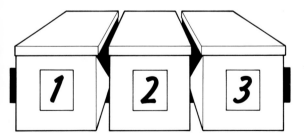

With these three kits, you've everything you'll need - apart from tap water - for routine maintenance procedures. If the manufacturer of your airbrush either supplies or recommends additional tools or cleaning items, obviously it makes sense to use those in accordance with instructions.

chapter five

CLEANING YOUR AIRBRUSH

Ignore this chapter at your peril. Cleanliness is the single most important aspect of owning an airbrush.

A LITTLE EFFORT, A LITTLE TIME

If you talk to an airbrush service agent, he'll tell you that 90 per cent of the airbrushes sent to him are simply blocked up or seized up through lack of regular, thorough cleaning. That's good business for him, but a poor reflection on the way some owners care for their instruments.

Quite simply, you cannot expect a finely-engineered tool to perform properly unless you treat it with due care and attention. That's not a lecture, it's a statement of fact. Happily, cleaning your airbrush correctly is relatively straightforward, requiring no great expertise, little expense and not a great deal of time - all the more reason why there can be no excuses for a slapdash attitude.

The case for cleaning your airbrush - and keeping it clean - really cannot be over-stated, and you couldn't do better than follow the example set by all the great chefs: do the washing-up (in our case, the airbrush cleaning) as you go along, and always leave your kitchen (airbrush) spotlessly clean at the end of every working day. Indeed, even if it's the middle of the night and bed is beckoning, you'll regret it next morning if you haven't cleaned your airbrush. It'll take you twice as long, and by having to 'scrub harder' as it were, you could damage your airbrush.

Obviously, cleaning methods will vary slightly depending on the type of airbrush you own; but your day-to-day cleaning programme should break down into three parts:

☐ Cleaning between colour changes

☐ End-of-session cleaning

☐ Further important cleaning

CLEANING BETWEEN COLOUR CHANGES

When you're switching colours, you need to flush out all paint residues both from the paint bowl or jar and from within the airbrush body.

Single-action airbrushes

Remove the colour jar, and return any useable amount of paint to its original pot. Rinse the jar with

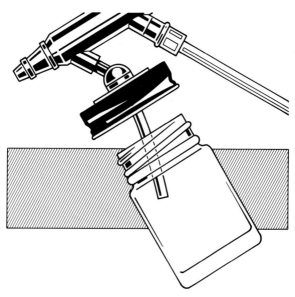

water or an appropriate cleaning fluid, then fill it with the same. Screw the jar back in position and spray the water/cleaning fluid through your airbrush onto a rag until all traces of the previous colour have disappeared. Remove the jar again, empty it and dry it carefully with a non-fibrous material. It is now ready to be refilled with the new colour.

Double-action airbrushes

To flush a double-action airbrush, first spray off any paint remaining in the cup or chamber into a jar or rag. Then fill the cup with water or a cleaning agent - it depends on the type of paint you're using - and spray it through your airbrush. You should now make sure the colour cup itself is spotlessly clean, using a cotton bud to wipe out any stubborn pigment - this doubles up as a drying method, too.

There is an alternative method of cleaning the colour cup which applies mainly to Japanese airbrushes. This is to retract, or remove, the needle, then fill the cup with water. Then put your finger or a piece of cloth over the end of your airbrush, and blow a little air through it. Your airbrush then 'gargles', cleaning out not only the cup but also the needle chamber.

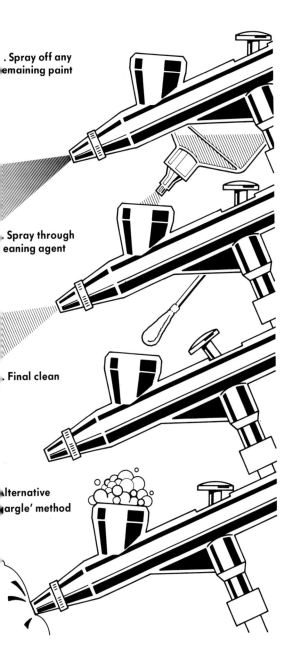

. Spray off any
emaining paint

. Spray through
eaning agent

. Final clean

Alternative
'gargle' method

END-OF-SESSION CLEANING

Just about the worst thing you can do to an airbrush is to put it away and leave it with paint remnants still inside it. After a very short while the paint will solidify and you'll have a terrible job trying to restore your airbrush to peak working condition next time you come to use it. So at the end of every working session, do yourself a favour by developing a cleaning habit. The first step is to flush out your airbrush as you would between colour changes: then continue with the following extra steps.

Single-action airbrushes

The most likely trouble-spot with a single-action airbrush is the paint channel and connection from the jar. It's hidden from view, but it's where paint is most likely to build up and lodge, so you must gain access to it and clean it.

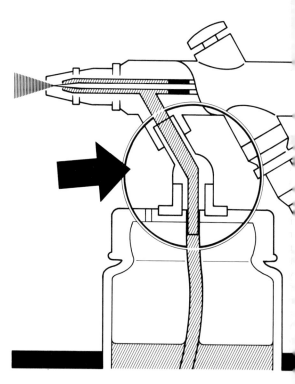

This is simply achieved by unscrewing the jar. The first thing to do is remove and clean the pipe itself. Then you should also inspect the hole through which the paint enters the airbrush body. If it's blocked or partially concealed, you should clean it with a needle. The next critical point is the air bleed hole in the jar lid: this should be clear at all times, so if it's not, go to work with a needle again.

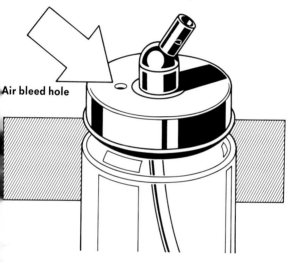

Air bleed hole

Double-action airbrushes

Your extra task here is to clean the needle. (If your airbrush is spluttering or blotting actually during use, you can try this remedy then, too).
First unscrew and remove the handle, and loosen the needle locking nut. Very gently remove the needle itself and check that it isn't damaged in any way (see next chapter for needle repair/replacement procedures). Now you can clean the needle in one of two ways. Either slide it gently across the palm of your hand, rotating it as you go, or draw it across a sheet of blotting paper in a cautious twisting manoeuvre. Finally, replace the needle, resting the shaft on your fingertip and steering it into place.
You can take the opportunity while the needle is out to coat it very lightly with petroleum jelly. This will aid the smooth movement of the needle within the airbrush body.

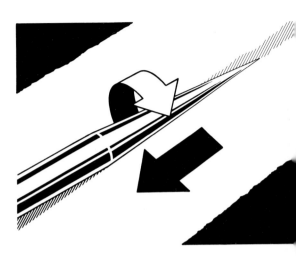

FURTHER IMPORTANT CLEANING

The steps outlined so far should be part of your daily,
routine life with the airbrush. They're not difficult and
they don't take long, and we're confident that you'll
quickly learn them and apply them without having to
refer back for instructions.

There is, however, one more important cleaning
procedure that you should carry out regularly -
cleaning the nozzle. You should do this, say, every
third or fourth time you use your airbrush. Airbrush
nozzle assemblies do vary quite extensively, and you
should study the next chapter in detail before you
attempt to dismantle your nozzle - the overlap
between nozzle maintenance and cleaning is
substantial. The full range of nozzle varieties is
discussed by airbrush type in Chapter 6, together
with comprehensive instructions for removing each
nozzle construction. Please read the section that
applies to your airbrush type before you set about
cleaning the nozzle.

Basically, there are three ways of cleaning nozzles.
The first is simply to fill your airbrush colour cup
with an approved cleaning agent, then blast it
through at full air pressure. This should work, but you
can't be fully sure as key nozzle components will
remain hidden from view. If you use this method, it's
advisable to remove the nozzle from time to time to
check all's well.

The second method is the overnight soak. This involves removing all metallic nozzle components, and leaving them in a tray of water or cleaning fluid overnight. (NB: never take what may seem to be an easy option and immerse your entire airbrush in water or cleaning fluid - parts will corrode and can easily be damaged beyond repair).

The third way is to clean your nozzle with a needle-like reamer. This instrument is supplied with some makes of airbrush and should be very gingerly poked into the nozzle to dislodge clogged paint. If your airbrush didn't come with one, you're best advised to clean the nozzle using the first or second method: not all nozzles are built to endure prodding and poking with a hard sharp object.

The overnight soak

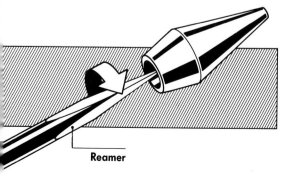

Reamer

chapter six

MAINTENANCE & TROUBLE-SHOOTING

Some basic steps,
some not so basic.
A simple rule: don't start
any repairs that you're
not wholly confident
you'll be able to finish.
That way, you won't
have to confront
a service agent with
a bag of bits.

GENERAL GUIDELINES

This chapter deals with maintenance and troubleshooting for the three major types of airbrush: single-action, double-action and turbo. While different manufacturers have slightly different designs for each type, you should be able to identify and match your particular model to our types and follow the step-by-step instructions without difficulty. Different manufacturers also call airbrush parts by different names. For instance, the terms 'lever' and 'trigger' are interchangeable. Consult the glossary for a full analysis of parts and their various names. While all major types of airbrush are covered here, basic spray guns have been omitted. Some more obscure models may also not fit directly into our categories, in which case you must follow the instructions drawn up by the manufacturers, or seek advice from the sales dealer. Likewise, if your airbrush was supplied with a special, purpose-designed tool-kit, maintenance procedures may be slightly different: adhere to those given by the manufacturer.

All said and done, there are three tips which you should take as your starting point when tackling maintenance and repairs.

1. Make sure you have a diagrammatic breakdown and parts list for your airbrush. All new airbrushes should be supplied with one, but if yours has been lost or destroyed, write to the manufacturer and request one. There's no point in relying on guesswork as to which part is which, and if you ever need spare parts you must be able to specify exactly what it is that you require, preferably by a reference number.

2. Choose a work-surface that is flat and well-lit, and when handling the airbrush work over something like the upturned lid of a shoe-box or biscuit tin. If you're dismantling your instrument, the last thing you want is to find a vital part missing when it comes to re-assembly. It helps to have a magnifying glass to hand too, for minutely inspecting components.

3. Most important of all, don't be afraid to admit when you're out of your depth. If you're not sure what's wrong and don't know how to fix it, our advice would be to take it in to an approved service agent. You can make some very expensive mistakes by taking stabs in the dark.

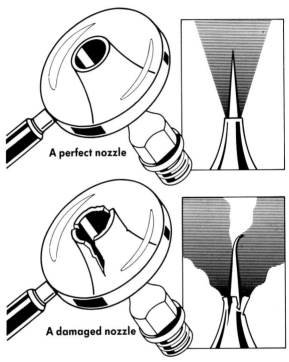

A perfect nozzle

A damaged nozzle

Equally there are two operating rules which help to prove the point that prevention is better than cure. Stick to these, and you'll go a long way towards eliminating the most common problems.

1. Never allow any paint into your airbrush that isn't of a milky consistency. If it's too thick or lumpy, it won't flow smoothly and at the very least, your airbrush will get hiccups.
2. Try not to raise the air pressure above 40 psi (2.6 bar). The components in air valves aren't built to withstand excessive pressures.

SINGLE-ACTION MAINTENANCE AND TROUBLESHOOTING

The good thing about single-action airbrushes is that they have only a limited number of components, so there is not very much that can go wrong. There are just four areas we need to look at, covering both external and internal mix models.

☐ **External mix nozzle/needle assembly**
☐ **Internal mix nozzle assembly**
☐ **Internal mix needle assembly**
☐ **Lever/air valve assembly**

The major difference between external and internal mix models is the construction of the nozzle assembly. If yours is an external mix, you'll notice that the nozzle incorporates a needle outside the airbrush body. If it's internal mix, you have a separate nozzle assembly and needle assembly, that operate together inside the airbrush body. These two different types of construction have their own maintenance requirements. Apart from that, the only other area you need to consider is the lever/air valve assembly which to all intents and purposes is the same for both models.

SINGLE ACTION CHECKLIST

External mix nozzle/needle assembly

CHECK that paint can flow freely through the assembly without blockages. Points to watch are the paint channel, the hole in the needle and the paint tip.

CHECK that any adjustment to alter the paint flow and spray pattern can be made — in other words make sure the paint tip hasn't seized up. Turn it clockwise to increase, anti-clockwise to decrease.

CHECK that air and paint seals are in good condition and not leaking.

CHECK that the needle is firmly secured by a set screw or lock-nut. If a set screw, make sure you have the correct wrench.

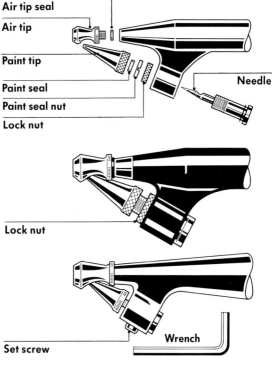

Air tip seal

Air tip

Paint tip

Needle

Paint seal

Paint seal nut

Lock nut

Lock nut

Set screw

Wrench

Internal mix nozzle assembly

CHECK that the paint tip is not damaged or blocked. If it is damaged, replace it. When it is screwed into the spray head, you should have an airtight seal, or the spray pattern will be affected.

CHECK that there is no paint build-up on the inside of the spray regulator — this could distort the spray pattern.

CHECK that the spray head washer is seated correctly and in good condition. It is important to keep an airtight seal between spray head and airbrush body.

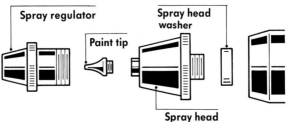

Spray regulator

Paint tip

Spray head washer

Spray head

Internal mix needle assembly

CHECK that the needle is not damaged or bent using a magnifying glass. If it is only slightly bent, try straightening it by gently rolling it across a flat hard surface such as a piece of glass. If this doesn't work, replace the needle.

CHECK that the amount of paint sprayed can be altered by turning the needle adjuster, and locking it with the needle chuck. It is important that both these parts move freely when required, and lubrication with petroleum jelly may be required.

CHECK that the needle bearing is not damaged or worn. This bearing stops paint travelling back up the needle, so if it is not in good condition you can have a messy problem. Most of these bearings are friction-fit, which can be pushed into place from the front of the airbrush body; make sure it is properly seated. If you have difficulty removing it, lightly twist a thin screw into it and pull.

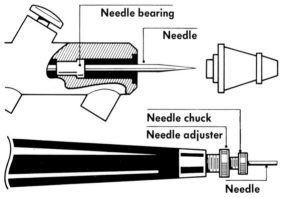

Needle bearing

Needle

Needle chuck
Needle adjuster

Needle

Lever/air valve assembly

CHECK that when you press the lever, the air valve opens allowing air to enter the airbrush body then exit via the air tip or head assembly. Release the lever, and make sure the air valve shuts off. If this isn't a simple on/off procedure — or if air is leaking from the assembly — check the internal components. The parts to concentrate on are the valve washer and valve spring. The spring should have enough tension to push up the plunger (thereby shutting off the air), and the washer should be seated correctly and not damaged or worn. The lever must then be able to move freely when pressed, pushing the plunger down to open the valve. Springs can be re-tensioned simply by stretching them. The lever can be lubricated, but if the washer or any other component is worn or damaged, you should replace it.

A common cause of air valve problems is foreign bodies entering the valve from the air supply, then lodging in the washer area. Finally, take care when dismantling the air valve assembly as the spring can cause the whole assembly to fly apart.

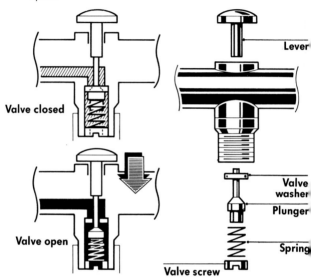

Lever

Valve closed

Valve open

Valve washer

Plunger

Spring

Valve screw

DOUBLE-ACTION MAINTENANCE AND TROUBLESHOOTING

Double-action models are sophisticated pieces of precision engineering, and certain repair work may be 'out of bounds' to all but the most skilled of owners. Certainly, many airbrush artists are quite happy to go as far as needle and nozzle replacement, but to leave bigger jobs to authorized service agents. That's worth considering.

There are four main areas that need attention, applicable to both fixed and independent double-action models.

☐ **Nozzle assembly**
☐ **Needle assembly**
☐ **Lever assembly**
☐ **Air valve assembly**

The area that varies the most across airbrush makes is the nozzle assembly. Some manufacturers prefer 'floating' nozzles, others incorporate 'screw-in' nozzles, and even within those sub-groups there is a good degree of design variance. To identify the precise nature of your nozzle, use our comprehensive guide. (page no 76)

Needles, levers and air valve assemblies differ less between makes, and in any case each of these components always fulfils the same function whatever the brand of airbrush. If the function is flawed, the root cause of the problem should be easily diagnosed. It's best to analyse the problem first, then trace it back to the part.

DOUBLE ACTION CHECKLIST

Nozzle assembly

CHECK which type of nozzle assembly you have, using our guide. Make sure the assembly is complete (look at the manufacturer's instructions or parts list) and that it has been put together correctly.

CHECK that the nozzle and other components are in perfect condition, without wear or damage, paint build-up or blockages. All these problems can affect the spray pattern. Make sure the needle sits perfectly in the nozzle.

CHECK for leaks in the airtight seals — air should only come out of the front of the nozzle. Do not submerge your airbrush in water to do this, just brush soapy water round the joint, press the lever for air and watch for bubbles. If there are any, and you are confident worn or missing parts are not causing the problem, try tightening the joint first. If this fails, apply a jointing compound or beeswax, but take care not to use too much and restrict the air and paint flow.

CHECK that when you remove or fit a screw-in nozzle, you are using the correct spanner. A new nozzle should fit tightly, but do be cautious because over-tightening will strip the threads or snap the nozzle. If the worst happens with a nozzle type that screws directly into the airbrush body, take it to a dealer to remedy the problem. It is all too easy to destroy the threads in the body beyond repair, especially if you start poking around trying to extract a stuck nozzle.

CHECK that you always have a spare nozzle to hand. If cleaning does not solve your nozzle problem, do not mess with it — replace it. Also keep a supply of nozzle washers and O rings handy, because these parts are easily lost. When you fit a new nozzle, it makes sense to fit a new needle at the same time.

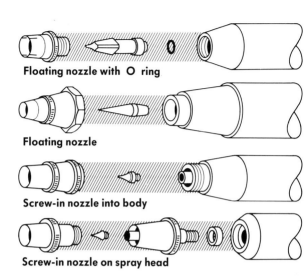

Floating nozzle with O ring

Floating nozzle

Screw-in nozzle into body

Screw-in nozzle on spray head

Needle assembly
CHECK the needle — see Single Action Internal Mix Needle assembly.

CHECK that the needle moves freely to and fro when operated by moving the lever. Your spray pattern will be affected if movement is restricted or if the needle does not sit properly in the nozzle. There are three suspect points for restriction. The first is the tip of the needle, where paint can accumulate — clean it. The second is the needle packing — if you have problems here, apply a light lubricant to the needle itself, then push the needle backwards and forwards by hand through the packing. If, at this stage, you notice paint working its way back up the needle, replace the packing. The packing is held in place by a packing screw which is visible when you remove the lever (see next section). Loosen this screw and take out the packing. Replace it with new packing, easing it in with the back of an old needle. Replace and tighten the packing screw, enabling the needle to move correctly through the new packing. A light lubricant may help. If the packing is a friction-fit bearing, refer to Single Action Internal Mix Needle Assembly. The third suspect point is around the needle return spring, which can seize up due to lack of cleaning and lubrication. Strip the assembly down, clean it and lubricate it, and re-tension the spring by stretching if required. If the needle movement is restricted by excessive wear or damage to any component, obviously that component must be replaced.

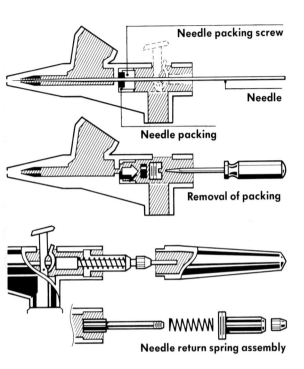

Needle packing screw

Needle

Needle packing

Removal of packing

Needle return spring assembly

Lever assembly

CHECK that the lever moves smoothly to its full extent, both down and back. If there is any restriction on movement, you have a problem and need to remove the lever assembly to get to the root of it. First, remove the needle and unscrew the needle return spring assembly to release any pressure on the lever. You should now be able to pull the lever out, although some types may require a twist. If your lever has a separate back or auxiliary lever, this should be removed too; be careful, it may fly out of its own accord. If, for any reason, you encounter difficulty removing your lever, get expert advice from your dealer. Once removed, inspect the lever for damage, paying particular attention to any pins or joints. If serious damage is evident, the only solution is a new lever. If it is just slightly bent, you could attempt to straighten it with a pair of pliers. Before replacing the lever, check the two points it comes into contact with: the air valve assembly and needle return spring assembly. The lever pushes down the air valve plunger to open the air valve, and you should ensure this function is working smoothly. Lubricate the area regularly, particularly if there is a piston or pin between the base of the lever and the air valve.

The needle return spring should function equally smoothly, with the lever pushing it back without problems. Again, the contact point should be regularly lubricated. When you replace your lever, make sure it sits neatly in the airbrush body; a common problem is positioning the back lever. First you should establish which way round it fits (consult the manufacturer's instructions), then insert it using a pair of tweezers. Hold it firmly in place while you tighten up the needle return spring assembly. Finally, replace the needle.

CHECK that the lever assembly is always clean and dry. If paint or any other liquid seeps in, the problems will start sooner or later.

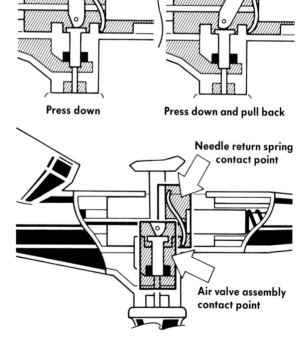

Lever

Back lever

Press down

Press down and pull back

Needle return spring contact point

Air valve assembly contact point

Air valve assembly
CHECK that when the lever operates the air valve, it is a clean on/off procedure. See Single Action Air Valve Assembly.

CHECK whether your air valve assembly is a pre-1980 diaphragm type. If it is, a recurring problem is probably an air leak around the lever area. You are advised to seek expert help from your dealer if this is the case; special tools are required for replacing the assembly. Post-1980 airbrushes feature an improved air valve, and special tools are not required.

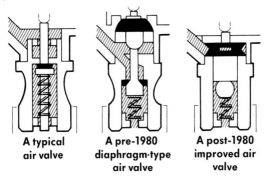

A typical	**A pre-1980**	**A post-1980**
air valve	**diaphragm-type**	**improved air**
	air valve	**valve**

TURBO MAINTENANCE AND TROUBLESHOOTING

The turbo is a highly-complex tool, and only authorized service agents should be entrusted with repairs that require a full strip-down. Limit yourself to simple maintenance and tuning, and you'll live a bit longer! It's interesting that every turbo has a character all of its own, and you should get to know yours well - an understanding, sympathetic handler can go a long way towards the well-being of a turbo. There are three areas which are useful in helping you to get to know the personality of your turbo.

☐ **Adjustments and tuning**
☐ **Maintenance and troubleshooting**
☐ **General hints**

TURBO CHECKLIST

Adjustments and tuning
CHECK the speed regulator screw, as this is the primary way of controlling the speed of the turbo needle. Turn it in (clockwise) to slow the needle, and out (anti-clockwise) to speed it up. To create fine lines, the rule of thumb is to slow the needle down, thus drawing only a little paint from the colour cup.

CHECK *the stipple adjuster, the primary way of controlling the volume of air through the air blast tube. Turn it in to decrease the amount of air, out to increase it. The greater the air, the greater the atomization of paint, so when the air is almost shut off you should be able to create a stipple effect.*

CHECK *the position of the colour cup and air blast tube — critical if you are aiming to achieve very fine lines. Loosen the colour cup screw, and slide the cup in or out until the tip of the needle projects beyond the needle bearing about $1/32$" to $1/64$". Re-tighten the screw. Next loosen the blast tube lock-nut and position the air blast jet just forward of the needle tip — $3/64$" is enough. The needle must be centred in the air stream, then the lock-nut fastened.*

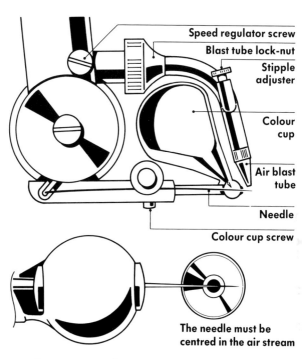

Speed regulator screw

Blast tube lock-nut

Stipple adjuster

Colour cup

Air blast tube

Needle

Colour cup screw

The needle must be centred in the air stream

Maintenance and troubleshooting

CHECK *when you obtain your turbo that you also have the name and address of an authorized service agent.*

CHECK *that your turbo is always spotlessly clean, especially the colour cup, needle, and grooves and holes along the paint path.*

CHECK that you can remove and replace the needle properly. Using a pair of tweezers, lift the front part of the needle (but not the tip) up and away from the needle guide screw. Next rotate it forward and lift it out of the walking arm and needle guide slots. Reverse the procedure to fit a new needle, which is supplied 'bowed' if it is direct from the factory. When fitted, the needle must reach all the way under the lip of the needle guide screw. If not, it could fly out like a most unpleasant missile. The needle guide screw should hold the needle snugly, without vibration.

CHECK any or all of the following if your turbo starts to spit or flood:

   a) The needle position
   b) The needle condition
   c) The distance and angle of air jet to needle
   d) The needle speed
   e) The air pressure
   f) The paint you are using

If they all seem to be correct or functioning properly, face up to it: the problem is probably operator error.

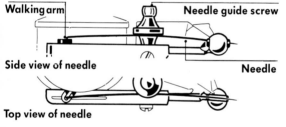

Walking arm | **Needle guide screw**

Side view of needle | **Needle**

Top view of needle

General Hints

1. Your turbo should always sound like a dentist's drill. If it chatters, or the sound dips and dives, something is wrong.

2. Never operate your turbo at a pressure above 45 psi. The needle might fly out.

3. Do not over-adjust the adjusting screws. They are brass and can be easily stripped.

4. To improve the turbo's capability for fine lines, sharpen and extend the taper of the needle using very fine emery paper.

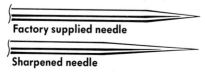

Factory supplied needle

Sharpened needle

chapter seven

LIVING WITH YOUR AIRBRUSH

Nobody should operate any mechanical instrument without proper regard for health and safety. Airbrushes are not inherently hazardous or dangerous, but they do call for some simple common sense.

SOMETHING IN THE AIR

When you're spraying, not every particle of paint ends up on your artwork. Those particles that escape into the air around you quickly build up into a fine mist which fills the atmosphere before settling as a paint dust in your studio. The problem can be particularly bad if you're using toxic substances such as enamels and lacquers, or when you're filling in a large background. It can be harmful to inhale this mist, and there are two ways in which you can contribute to your own well-being: you can control your working environment, and you can protect yourself.

CONTROLLING YOUR WORKING ENVIRONMENT

The smaller the room you work in, the less space there is for the mist to diffuse. So think carefully about the size of the room you choose as your studio, and certainly make sure it is no smaller than 4 square yards/3.6 square metres. If the weather allows, you should also keep a window open all the time you're working, and leave it open for an hour or so after you've stopped. That's not always practical, so the best course of action is to fit an extractor fan which can be used whether it's blowing a gale or freezing outside. The types that are often found in kitchens are fine, and there are models that can be fitted into an outside wall or into panes of glass. It may be a nuisance, but make sure the on/off switch is in a handy position: the switching-on habit is much easier to acquire if the switch is staring you in the face when you sit down to work, as opposed to a leg-stretch away.

If you're particularly lazy or forgetful, there is an alternative! A range of desk-top extractor fans has been introduced, specifically for airbrush artists. These models purify and recirculate the air around your desk, sucking it in by electric-powered fans and processing it through a filter. You do have to change the filter occasionally, but otherwise these easy-to-use, convenient extractors provide an effective, practical solution.

There's one more device you should also consider, again specially designed for airbrush users. It's a plastic canister containing a filtration system, and it's particularly handy when you come to empty, clean or change the colour in your airbrush. Instead of blasting away into the atmosphere around you, you should clear your airbrush by spraying into the canister which will absorb the left-over paint. These ingenious devices can sit on a desk, they don't take up much room and the designer deserves credit for coming up with something that not only works well, but also looks good.

Again, there's an alternative, and that is to improvise and make your own cheap and cheerful version. Fill a small cardboard box with tissues or cotton wool, seal the box carefully with tape, then cut a small hole in one side that's just big enough to poke the front of your airbrush in. You can empty your spray into this, but it won't last forever. When you feel the box has ceased to absorb paint fully, throw it away and make another one. This isn't a perfect solution and the professional, purpose-built device is preferable, but anything that helps to cut down the amount of paint loose in the atmosphere just has to be a good thing.

Plastic canister filtration system

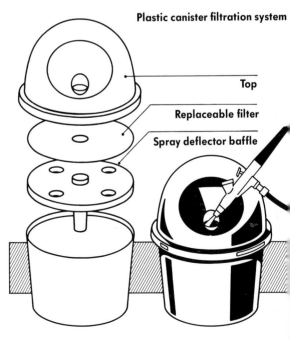

Top

Replaceable filter

Spray deflector baffle

PROTECTING YOURSELF

We're not going to sit on the fence: we believe you should wear a mask when airbrushing, to prevent inhalation of paint particles.

There are many different types of industrial mask that cover both mouth and nose, and you should try out a few to find which is most comfortable for you. If you use only water-based paints like inks and watercolours, a light dust mask should suffice. If you use toxic paints - enamels, lacquers or oils - you need a filter respirator mask. As soon as you mention paint, the man behind the counter at the industrial supplies store may try to sell you a full head mask, as used by vehicle resprayers: you don't need to go that far.

Wearing a mask can seem tiresome initially, but it's like wearing spectacles - it seems strange the first week, you're mildly conscious of it the second, and you cease to notice it thereafter. Given that you'll only have to wear your mask for short periods, and probably not every day, it isn't such a big deal to make the effort. It's worth it.

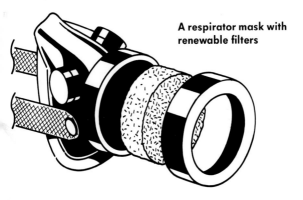

A respirator mask with renewable filters

LAST WORD

Never aim your airbrush, full or empty, at any part of the human body. Tempting as it may be to body-paint your partner, don't: you could easily end up with a partner who's only got one of something we're meant to have two of. Seriously, use your common sense about health and safety, and only use your airbrush as it is intended to be used.

Note Different airbrush manufacturers - and indeed airbrush users in different countries - often refer to the same component by different names. The lever, for instance, can also be called the button or trigger. Where possible, alternative terms are shown in this glossary.

Abrasives Useful for removing any corrosion that may build up on airbrush components. Usually in the form of metal polish.

Acrylic A fast-drying plastic paint that produces a tough waterproof finish. Can be used whole or mixed with water.

Adaptor Almost any airbrush can be linked to any air source by use of a threaded adaptor. Multi-outlet adaptors - manifolds - are available enabling up to five airbrushes to be run off one compressor. See also Quick-disconnect connector.

Airbrush An air-powered instrument which propels a spray of atomized paint at a surface. Various models are available from simple spray guns to sophisticated precision turbo-driven types.

Air can Propellant cans of pressurized liquid gas that can be linked to an airbrush and used as a power source.

Air hose (Air line) Used to provide an airtight link between the air source and airbrush. Hoses are available in clear plastic, braided rubber and curly coil, in various lengths.

Air seal See O ring

Air trap See Moisture trap.

Air valve The assembly that is fitted into the body of the airbrush above the air line connection. It is operated by the trigger and controls the air flow.

Art paper A smooth, almost glossy paper that is ideal for airbrushing onto. Art board is board-backed version of art paper.

Atomization The point at which a liquid paint becomes a spray, achieved when compressed air is introduced to the paint.

Automatic compressor A motor-powered machine that generates and stores compressed air, dispensing it at a constant pressure. The most reliable air source for use with an airbrush.

Bar The unit of atmospheric pressure. 1 bar equals 14.5 psi (pounds per square inch).

Bowl See Colour cup.

Button See Lever.

Car tyre A basic, cheap air source that can be used as an alternative to the compressor.

CO2 cylinder A large air cylinder that can be used as an alternative to the compressor.

Colour cup The receptacle that holds the paint before it is sprayed through the airbrush. Colour cups take various forms: they can be integral bowls mounted on the top or to the side of the airbrush, recessed slits on top of the airbrush, or detachable jars attached to the underside. See also Reservoir and Well.

Compressed air Air that is kept at a higher pressure than that found in the atmosphere. In the airbrush this performs the function of atomizing the paint, and propelling it.

Diaphragm assembly A valve and lever system found in some independent double-action airbrushes.

Diaphragm compressor A compressor in which a fan sucks air in, a diaphragm compresses it and then syphons it into the air hose. Prone to 'pulsing '.

Direct compressor See Diaphragm compressor.

Double-action airbrush The type of airbrush with which the operator can control the flow of both paint and air.

External atomization This occurs in the more basic types of airbrush: air and paint meet outside the body of the airbrush, atomizing in the air.

Fixed double-action airbrush Less versatile than their independent double-action counterparts, these airbrushes deliver paint and air at a pre-set ratio. The lever only goes in one direction, so paint/air ratios cannot be varied while spraying.

Fluid tip See Nozzle.

Freehand airbrushing The art of spraying without the use of masks of any sort.

Gouache A water-based paint recognized for its opacity. It produces strong colours that dry to a matt finish.

Gradation The technique of spraying to achieve a subtle transition from one colour or tone through to another.

Gravity feed The method by which paint is fed into the airbrush body by gravity. The colour cup in gravity-fed airbrushes is mounted either on top or to the side of the airbrush body.

Independent double-action airbrush The airbrush type preferred by most users. The lever moves in two directions: down for air, and back for paint. Thus the artist can control both the amount of paint and the volume of air, in any given proportion.

Ink A liquid colour medium - it cannot really be defined as a paint - which holds pigments in suspension. There are two types, waterproof and non-waterproof, and both are ideal for airbrushing.

Internal atomization This occurs when paint and air are combined within the airbrush nozzle. The resultant spray is of a better consistency and quality than that produced by external atomization.

Jointing compound The most effective material for plugging leaks and achieving an airtight seal in your airbrush/air hose/air source system.

Lever (Button, Trigger) The finger-operated control on the top of an airbrush that dictates the flow of air and paint through the airbrush.

Mask Anything which prevents the spray actually reaching the surface being sprayed. Purpose-designed masking film is most generally used by artists, but masks can take any form - a leaf, a feather, a paper clip.

Moisture trap (Air trap) Moisture traps can be either built-in or bolted on to compressors. They prevent the moisture that naturally collects in a compressor from creeping up the air hose, and into the airbrush. Unchecked, these beads of moisture will cause your airbrush to spatter.

Needle The needle is perhaps the most critical of all airbrush components: it controls the flow of paint through the airbrush, transporting it to the airbrush head. It is a delicate part, which needs regular cleaning and inspection. The needle is locked into position with a needle locking nut (needle chuck).

Needle packing Fitted inside the airbrush body, these glands help the needle to move smoothly, while at the same time preventing paint being pushed back into the handle. Needle packing glands are sometimes known as needle bearings, needle gland washers, or paint seal.

Nozzle (Fluid tip) The nozzle is the casing that contains and protects the needle tip. In airbrush models that work on the principle of internal atomization, it is also where the paint and air meet and combine. One part of the nozzle assembly is the needle cap, which is variously known as the spray regulator or air cap.

O Ring (Air seal, Washer) A small circular washer made from rubber, neoprene or teflon.

Overspray When an airbrush is directed at a point on the paper, inevitably some particles of paint fall away from that point. This overspray is often deliberately used by airbrush artists to create effects.

PSI Pounds per square inch, the unit of measurement for compressed air.

Piston compressor The type of compressor in which an electric motor powers a piston which compresses the air.

Propellant Any air source that is used to power an airbrush - the air can, the car tyre, the CO_2 cylinder and the various types of compressor.

Pulsing The uneven, spasmodic flow of air produced by diaphragm compressors. This 'heartbeat' can cause spattering.

Quick-disconnect connectors A development of the adaptor. These connectors operate on a 'pull-me, push-me' principle, and can be fitted at either end of the air hose. The air automatically shuts off when they are disconnected.

Reamer Supplied with certain makes of airbrush, a reamer is a sharp, thin needle-like tool for cleaning airbrush nozzles. Use carefully.

Regulator A fitment to a compressor that allows the operator to adjust the air pressure. Some are combined in one unit with a moisture trap.

Reservoir The sealed steel tank in storage compressors, where the compressed air is maintained. The term is also sometimes applied to the recessed colour cups found on certain makes of airbrush.

Return spring The component responsible for the smooth return of the needle when the lever is released.

Single-action airbrush The type of airbrush which expels only a pre-set amount of paint - the lever only controls the air flow. On certain models, you can adjust the paint level but you must stop spraying to do so.

Solvent Any substance that can be used to remove solidified paint from the passages of the airbrush. Different paints require different solvents. Water, for instance, will not remove oils and lacquers, which require special solvents.

Spatter A coarsely-textured spray, achieved by spraying a lot of paint with a little air. The spatter effect is a stock-in-trade of the airbrush artist.

Spatter cap A device which can be fitted to some airbrushes in place of the nozzle cap, to create a spatter effect.

Spidering An unsightly splodge of colour, frequently found at the end of an airbrushed line. The problem is commonly caused by an excess of either paint, air or both.

Spray The atomized jet of paint propelled at a surface by an airbrush.

Stipple Similar to a spatter, only grainier in texture. The even, small dot pattern can be created by lowering the air pressure and spraying from a further distance than normal. Alternatively, stipple effects can be created by hand with a paintbrush.

Storage compressor Any compressor that generates and then stores air, as opposed to pumping it directly into the airbrush. Storage compressors generally supply good quality, even air flow.

Suction feed The method by which paint is drawn into the airbrush by a suctional force created by high pressure air forcing a drop in the ambient air pressure in the colour cup. In suction-fed airbrushes, the colour cup usually takes the form of a jar positioned beneath the airbrush body.

Tank compressor See Storage compressor.

Trigger See Lever.

Turbo airbrush The complex, challenging turbine-driven airbrush which, in expert hands, is capable of producing finely-detailed work.

Washer See O ring.

Watercolour A transparent paint, which can be diluted with water. Ideal for use with the airbrush.

Well A commonly-used name for the colour cup that takes the form of a recessed slit on top of the airbrush - otherwise referred to as a reservoir.

ACKNOWLEDGEMENTS

Series editor: Judy Martin
Design and art direction: Nigel Osborne
Design assistant: Peter Serjeant
Artwork: Peter Owen